THE MENTEE'S GUIDE
TO MENTORING

Dr. Norman H. Cohen

sachusetts

Published by:

HRD Press
22 Amherst Road
Amherst, MA 01002
1-800-822-2801 (U.S. and Canada)
413-253-3488
413-253-3490 (fax)
www.hrdpress.com

Printed in Canada

ISBN 0-87425-494-9

Cover design by Eileen Klockars
Editorial services by Robie Grant
Production services by CompuDesign

CONTENTS

Introduction   1

    Purpose   1

    Organization and Topic Selection   2

    Respect for Mentee Interpersonal Style   3

    The Informed Mentee and the Mentor   4

1. The Purpose of the Mentoring Relationship   5

    Perspectives on Mentoring   5

    Importance of Realistic Expectations   5

    Dealing with Time Constraints   6

    Enhanced Insight Prior to Participation   7

2. The Matching Process   9

    Methods of Matching Participants   9

    Mentee Investment in the Match   10

    Guidelines for Selecting or Accepting a Mentor   13

    Deciding Whether to Terminate a Match   14

    Mentor–Mentee Flashpoints   14

    Two Approaches to Resolving Conflict   15

    The Productive Use of Time: Understanding and Working
        within the Boundaries of Mentoring   15

3. **Maintaining a Mentee Journal**   19

    The Journal and Its Uses   19

    1. An Accurate Source of Information   19

    2. An Ongoing Register of Ideas   20

4. **The Policy of Using Mentors as References**   21

    Preliminary Considerations   21

    Reasons for the No-Use Policy   21

    The Issue of Trust   22

    Reference Policies and Mentee Decisions   24

5. **Understanding the Complete Mentor Role**   25

    The Mentor Role   25

    The Value of the Concept for Mentees   26

    Knowing and Doing—The Need for Application   26

    Self-Advocates, Not Imitators   26

    The Six Dimensions of the Mentor Role   27

      Figure 1. *Behavioral Profile of an Effective Mentee*   28

6. **The Phases of Mentoring**   31

    Significance for Mentees   31

    The Need for Flexibility   32

    Shift in Responsibility   33

7. **Mentee Responses to Mentoring Behavior**   35

    Introduction   35

    Dimension 1—Relationship   35

      Purpose and Definition   35

      Mentor Behaviors   36

      Key Point—TRUST   36

      Underlying Structure   36

      Perception of Trust   36

Rational Involvement 37

Assumption of Trust 38

Dimension 2—Information 39

Purpose and Definition 39

Mentor Behaviors 39

Key Point—ADVICE 40

Seek Tailored Advice 41

A Detailed Mentee Picture 42

Eliciting the Facts—Interpersonal Style 42

Mentee Preparation of Facts 43

Dimension 3—Facilitative 44

Purpose and Definition 44

Mentor Behaviors 45

Key Point—ALTERNATIVES 45

Mentor as Reality Check 46

Advantages of Abbreviated Review 46

Real versus Imagined 47

Referral 47

Exploring Problems within the Mentoring Model 48

Review of Objectives 49

Resources to Meet Demands of the Journey 49

Dimension 4—Confrontative 51

Purpose and Definition 51

Mentor Behaviors 51

Key Point—CHALLENGE 51

Mentee Awareness of Constructive Behaviors 53

Essential Value 54

Confrontation Is Not Therapy 55

Challenge 55

Self-Limiting Mentee Behavior 56

Timing and Selection 57

Dimension 5—Mentor Model   58

   Purpose and Definition   58

   Mentor Behaviors   58

   Key Point—MOTIVATION   59

   Selective Self-Disclosure   59

   References to the Past   60

   Perception of Risk   61

   New Risk versus Old Risk   62

   View of the Mentor as Role Model   63

Dimension 6—Employee Vision   64

   Purpose and Definition   64

   Mentor Behaviors   64

   Key Point—INITIATIVE   64

   A Realistic Interpretation of Vision   66

   Mentees as Independent Adult Learners   67

   Relevance of a Network   67

   Change and Transition   68

Conclusion   69

  Mentor and Mentee Preparation   69

  Remembering the Mentee's Responsibilities   69

Appendices   71

  Use of the Appendices   71

  Appendix A. Summary of the Complete Mentor Role   72

  Appendix B. Behavioral Profile of an Effective Mentee   73

INTRODUCTION

Purpose

The Mentee's Guide to Mentoring provides mentees with a solid foundation for understanding the mentoring process and their responsibilities as participants in that process. Its primary purpose is to offer practical advice that orients mentees to two vital components of any successful mentoring experience:

1. The art of establishing and maintaining productive interpersonal communication with mentors

2. The mentee's acceptance of an *active, collaborative* role in learning

Mentees who are knowledgeable about these components can better grasp the dynamics of the one-to-one mentoring relationship and thus are more likely to make substantial contributions to the process. They are prepared for what the mentor model of learning requires of them, including:

- *Realistic expectations.* Mentors must make a professional commitment to helping mentees achieve positive outcomes; however, they are not solo practitioners, and mentees should not expect them to assume total responsibility for the learning experience.

- *Mutual effort/Collaboration.* The success of a mentor–mentee relationship depends in large part on such effort. Even the most experienced and dedicated mentor must receive a conscientious, *reciprocal* response from the mentee if the process is to yield beneficial results.

▪ *Readiness for challenge and learning.* Mentees who are cognizant of the challenges and potential of the one-to-one approach to education are in a favorable position to *maximize* their learning opportunities with mentors and, as creative learners, achieve significant individual development.

In imparting to mentees this enhanced perception of their role and an awareness of their obligations to the mentoring process, *The Mentee's Guide* unites the conceptual and the pragmatic, facilitating a more efficient and effective use of time and energy on the part of mentor and mentee alike.

Organization and Topic Selection

The guidebook is divided into seven chapters and includes two appendices. Each chapter focuses on an important facet of the mentoring experience, from the purpose of the mentoring relationship (Chapter 1) to mentee responses to mentoring behavior (Chapter 7). The appendices provide the user with outlines of both the mentor's role and the corresponding effective mentee behavior, for reference before and after mentoring sessions. As a complete work, the book represents a *unified* approach to mentoring, based on the assumption that mentees need both conceptual explanations *and* practical guidance if they are to benefit directly from the mentoring experience.

Given that assumption, the general criteria for topic selection have called for information and guidelines that (1) will be immediately useful to mentees, and (2) will enable mentees to do the following:

▪ Understand the essential purpose and attainable goals of sponsored programs

▪ Comprehend the responsibilities of persons who have been properly oriented and trained to function in the complete mentor role

▪ Learn and apply the interpersonal skills typically required of both mentees and mentors

▪ Recognize the realistic possibilities for learning usually offered by face-to-face interaction

▪ Anticipate internal and external problems normally inherent in mentoring-based development initiatives

- Fulfill their own obligation to respond as collaborative participants in their contact with mentors

- Identify specific actions they can pursue as independent learners during the evolving phases of mentoring

In using the guidebook, mentees should thus find the comprehensive direction and overview they need to prepare for, and to successfully meet, the challenges of the mentoring process.

Respect for Mentee Interpersonal Style

Another important assumption underlying this work is that the mentor will take a balanced, discerning view of the mentee and his or her needs. The mentor should not only welcome and accept each mentee's unique interpersonal style (both verbal and nonverbal) but also, as a responsible professional, offer productive assistance in those cognitive, behavioral, and affective areas that could prove beneficial to the mentee's career and educational pursuits.

On their part, mentees should expect mentors to encourage them to express their personalities; yet as adult learners, they should also be open to constructive feedback on their particular ideas, beliefs, actions, and attitudes. Of course, mentees must never allow themselves to be treated as if they need to *become* someone else in order to increase their interpersonal competency or to engage in meaningful self-development, though fortunately such mistreatment is an unlikely possibility.

Mentees can expect similar respect for their interpersonal styles from *The Mentee's Guide*. As its title indicates, the work is indeed meant to *guide* them, to generally show the way via the knowledge and experience of a seasoned traveler. Its intent is *not* to patronize mentees by instructing them in how to conduct themselves according to a hard and fast set of acceptable criteria. The relationship that characterizes adult mentoring programs is far too broad-based and complex for such prescriptions. Consequently, mentees will not find standard dialogue examples in this book, suggesting that they approach the mentoring process as if they were actors who have memorized the lines of a play and then rehearsed their responses. Rather, they will find a clear, sensible orientation to mentor–mentee interaction, one that emphasizes their role as responsible and collaborative participants.

The Informed Mentee and the Mentor

Obviously, mentors who are properly trained to function in the mentor role will be more apt to provide the type of mentoring environment that genuinely contributes to the career, training, and academic development of mentees. In most cases, mentees can assume that when *The Mentee's Guide* is officially distributed as part of the orientation program, their mentors have also been exposed to other published information. It is certainly appropriate to inquire about the level of training provided to mentors, especially from the perspective of informed mentees who are attempting to engage their own mentors as collaborative adult learners.

Mentees who interact with well-intentioned but less knowledgeable or skilled mentors can still initiate relevant actions to advance the learning curve by personally committing to the creation of meaningful one-to-one relationships. In these situations, as in all the varieties of mentor–mentee involvement, it is critical that mentees attempt to function as *active* rather than passive learners.

Chapter 1

THE PURPOSE OF THE MENTORING RELATIONSHIP

Perspectives on Mentoring

Mentoring programs can serve purposes both social and individual. It is useful to consider the mentoring model as serving complementary agendas, so that the benefits obtained by mentees are consistent with the goal of adding value to the larger culture in which the mentor–mentee relationship occurs.

Organizations that fall into the broad categories of business and government, and nonprofit enterprises as well, can enjoy gains in productivity from the increasing competency and confidence of their sponsored mentees, who continue to perform as valuable members of the workforce. Others, such as educational institutions that conduct programs for students, can incorporate the mentoring model of learning into the larger mission of educating more personally fulfilled and socially concerned citizens.

From the unique perspective of the mentee, however, the organization's principal reason for establishing a mentoring program should be the advantages that accrue to the adult learner—the mentee. This is a valid view of mentoring, but it comes with an obligation: Mentees who expect to be primary beneficiaries must also be prepared to assume considerable responsibility for actively pursuing and obtaining all the opportunities for professional and personal development offered by their mentors and the resources of the programs.

Importance of Realistic Expectations

Mentees who enter into mentoring relationships with realistic expectations can more fully engage their mentors. Aware mentees can accelerate the learning curve by initiating productive dialogues that help mentors assist them more effectively with a multitude of concerns. These include such essential tasks as:

■ Developing coherent educational and professional goals

■ Engaging in career, training, and academic planning

■ Undertaking realistic and continuing reviews of options

■ Arriving at decisions based on pragmatic assessments of talents and resources

■ Devising workable strategies to solve problems

■ Following through with decisive actions to fulfill specific objectives

■ Guiding the general development of intellectual, technical, and behavioral proficiencies needed to meet the requirements of work performance standards, technical certification, and academic criteria

In addition to exploring how mentors can help them with the more cognitive dimensions of learning, mentees should keep in mind that mentors can serve as valuable sources of personal support. As established workplace reference points, mentors are often able to provide the critical psychological and emotional stability that some mentees need to manage difficult transitions and to skillfully negotiate complex changes.

Dealing with Time Constraints

For many mentees, the learning opportunity offered by the mentoring experience occurs at a critical juncture in their lives. Since most institutionally sponsored programs operate under the pressure of time constraints, it is vital that participants efficiently utilize mentoring interaction, activities, and projects.

Mentees must recognize that even when mentors are truly striving to fulfill mutually agreed to learning objectives, they cannot always meet on a consistent basis because of the intense demands of the contemporary work environment. For example, mentors are typically able to schedule only two to four sessions each month. The practical opportunity for daily or even weekly contact specifically dedicated to mentor–mentee interaction, while certainly a feasible option, is more often the exception than the norm.

There also can be great variety in the administrative and personnel resources that are allocated. Official mentor–mentee involvement is usually planned to run about twelve months, although the time span for specific pairings can range from six months to three years, depending on the goals and support for the program.

Both mentor and mentee should therefore attempt to plan and conduct mentoring activities that ensure they achieve the maximum learning possible within the time available.

Enhanced Insight Prior to Participation

Mentees can definitely profit from entering into mentoring relationships with an enhanced insight into their shared responsibility for the learning process. Savvy mentees come prepared to respond to their mentors in a constructive and timely manner, and so are able to accelerate their progress and enrich the program's time frame. Their readiness for the mentoring experience is grounded in two perceptual basics:

1. A mature understanding of mentoring's potential for talent development

2. A proper respect for the necessary boundaries and limitations of the one-to-one model of learning

This enlightened approach, in facilitating realistic expectations for the process and a sensitive appreciation of time constraints, is thus a critical variable that promotes the intelligent involvement and personal accomplishment of the participants.

Chapter 2

THE MATCHING PROCESS

Methods of Matching Participants

There are numerous methods for arranging the pairings between mentors and mentees. Possibilities range from working out the basic logistics of "who can meet when" to conducting rather elaborate procedures for finding the "ideal" match, including various compatibility and interest tests. The specific selection will depend on the ideas and experiences of the program administrators as well as the availability of financial and staff resources.

It is important for mentees to realize that different philosophies are usually the driving force behind the more complex efforts to ensure a proper pairing. Some program directors, for example, view the mentor–mentee match as a highly critical component of the mentoring relationship, and consider age, gender, ethnicity, and religion to be very important variables. Other factors, such as personal comfort level, similarity of occupational interests, and personality profile are also considered relevant to arranging a "good fit" between mentors and mentees.

Behind the more carefully worked out approach, of course, is the belief that the more familiar the participants' backgrounds, the greater the chance they will be personally and professionally compatible. Here the powerful operational assumption is that by satisfying as many mentor and mentee preferences as is feasible, program administrators will increase the probability of producing a successful face-to-face relationship and, therefore, a productive learning experience overall.

Mentees must recognize, however, that other administrators regard the matching process as a limited-choice event. While they may agree with the ideal-match concept in theory, such administrators will honestly state that real mentoring programs operate in less than perfect situations, with a relatively small number of organizational personnel volunteering to serve as mentors; therefore, although they would like to honor all of the participants' priorities, they are not in a position to comply with such requests. The inescapable fact is that "ideal matches" are simply beyond the scope of most programs, and cannot be realistically regarded as a desirable option.

Actually, not all program managers are convinced that familiarity and individual preferences are the most promising guidelines for mentoring programs to follow. Some believe that random pairing is as effective as more complicated matching methods because dissimilar partners, in experiencing genuinely different viewpoints, tend to learn more from each other than similar ones do. Such managers clearly assume that mentors and mentees will benefit from a match that enables them to develop flexibility and adaptability, qualities that are vital characteristics of mature adults.

Mentee Investment in the Match

The significance administrators attach to matching may also reflect prior mentee and mentor feedback. In situations where participants have expressed little dissatisfaction with the process, mentees may find that administrators are unlikely to commit special resources to an agenda that interests only a small percentage of the group.

Mentees who firmly believe that, for them, more finely tuned matching endeavors are justified should be prepared to clarify such issues with administrators at the earliest stage of their contact with the program. In addition to reviewing such concerns as "personality" compatibility, mentees should reflect on their reasons for engaging in the mentoring relationship as adult learners.

Organization and Mentee Agendas

Programs sponsored by organizations normally have their own stated agendas, such as helping employees develop into increasingly productive and satisfied members of the workforce and even advance into positions of junior and senior leadership. Mentees typically find themselves quite comfortable with the mentoring model of learning, even if they have highly specific personal and professional reasons, because the goals of the program, the mentors, and the mentees are complementary.

Mentees usually discover that their ideas about self-development harmonize with the goals announced by program administrators. Often mentees will also find that they share a relatively similar agenda for requesting mentors, one that can be broken down into four basic areas:

1. An interest in obtaining concrete guidance from someone who is experienced and knowledgeable about selecting career, training, and academic routes

2. A desire to participate in dialogues and activities that offer mentees challenges and opportunities to explore their own plans, ideas, and beliefs, including networking

3. Concerns about gaining insight into the "inner workings" of the organizational culture, especially with regard to issues of recognition and promotion

4. An expectation of holistic support from mentors—intellectual, psychological, and emotional

Mentee Preferences and Goals

Some mentees prefer certain types of mentoring styles over others. For instance, a mentee might indicate that he or she would most benefit from working with a mentor whose interpersonal style focuses on accuracy and completeness of information, concrete guidance based on expressed goals, and direct application of facts to the mentee's unique situation.

Whether or not mentees enter the program with clearly defined objectives, some also prefer to limit their discussions to the intellectual, content-centered aspect of mentor–mentee interaction. In general, they initially perceive only a minimum need to examine psychological issues or to seek emotional support relevant to the workplace. Mentees should consider this more "limited" expectation valid within the boundaries of mentoring and be prepared to express their viewpoints. Mentors, of course, are obliged to honor their mentees' sensible and focused preferences.

Moreover, mentees should note that even though the announced program objectives often include a reference to a "supportive" (and not just factual)

experience, they should not feel *compelled* to engage in the more psychological and emotional dimensions as recipients of a sponsored learning experience. If there are any questions about the exact obligations that mentees are agreeing to meet, then they should inquire about the details of their commitment—earlier rather than later.

By contrast, other mentees, in addition to pursuing the intellectual facet, are seeking the opportunity not only to openly explore their career and educational options, but also to directly test their own views and opinions —anticipating that the affective dimension will be an integral component of their interpersonal contact. Sometimes these mentees prefer a mentoring approach that is less dominated by the "facts" and more balanced; they expect their mentors to examine both the cognitive and emotional dimensions as relevant factors in the workplace.

The Limits of Prediction

Obviously, mentees cannot see into the future and predict with complete accuracy the changes they will undergo as a result of the mentoring experience; therefore, they should not regard their initial objectives as a fixed compass that strictly determines the acceptable topics and concerns for the entire journey. In fact, it is to be expected that some mentees will not define *all* of their self-development goals until they have gained more experience, possibly through an extension or evolution of their early objectives.

Communicating Preferences to Mentors

Mentees should communicate to their mentors as clearly as possible the current state of their preferences, and should directly ask for mentors' opinions if their proposed agendas change during the mentoring relationship. In the majority of cases, mentors will welcome the chance to expand beyond the facts into other areas of mentee concern related to career and educational issues.

However, in opening the interpersonal door somewhat wider to accommodate other concerns, mentees should never feel obligated to discuss topics that cause them genuine distress, especially if they also believe that such points are outside the proper domain of the mentor model of learning.

Accepting the Limitations of Mentors

Finally, mentees must realize that even the most skilled and conscientious mentor cannot be "all things to all people." Consequently, mentees should be prepared to accept their mentors' sincere efforts to provide meaningful assistance, and receive it as graciously as it is offered. Even the most accomplished mentor may be unable, though not necessarily unwilling, to meet *all* expectations.

Guidelines for Selecting or Accepting a Mentor

From the mentee's perspective, the most suitable mentor is someone who meets the criteria essential to promoting meaningful learning in the workplace. When initially reviewing the important factors of selection or acceptance, mentees should consider the mentor's ability to do the following:

1. Schedule regular one-to-one sessions

2. Engage in constructive interpersonal dialogues, including offering productive feedback (criticism) and sharing personal and professional experiences relevant to issues of direct concern to mentees

3. Create specific strategies designed to accommodate each individual's unique pursuit of career and educational goals

4. Arrange for attendance (as a guest) at a variety of meetings that offer exposure to the dynamics of different groups within the organization

5. Use their network of professional contacts to provide access to other staff and offices

6. Act as a resource of ideas and information

Naturally, it may take time for mentees to determine whether a mentor can fulfill these expectations. Realistic assessments usually require more than a few mentoring sessions, and too hasty a judgment can result in an unwarranted request for a replacement. Moreover, mentor behaviors that are annoying at first, or a mentor's apparent commitment to ideas and beliefs that are very different from the mentee's, could turn out to be relatively minor distractions or unimportant concerns after sufficient mentor–mentee contact. Mentees should thus be alert to the danger of attaching too much importance to superficial appearances.

Deciding Whether to Terminate a Match

Typically, for the length of the mentoring program both mentor and mentee will fulfill their responsibilities and remain dedicated to achieving the announced goals of the mentoring model of learning. Still, problems related to mentor or mentee responsibility can develop, and mentees should be prepared to deal with them and raise any concerns openly with mentors.

If a major problem develops fairly early—especially the proverbial "personality clash"—then mentees should consider discussing the issue with the mentor *and* the program administrator. In such cases, mentees need to remain calm and nonjudgmental. Both the mentee and the mentor must remember that such problems will occasionally arise, and that for whatever (probably complex) reason the pair is unable to forge a constructive interpersonal relationship, the matter should not be immediately interpreted as an indication of bad faith on someone's part.

Mentor–Mentee Flashpoints

There are a number of mentor–mentee flashpoints that can disrupt the opportunity for learning. Foremost among them are serious differences of opinion about or resulting from one or more of these issues:

- The specific minimal level of commitment the mentor should demonstrate in assisting the mentee
- The extent of mentee obligation to pursue mentor-initiated or -preferred projects
- Divergent views of professional obligations to the organization
- Clearly opposite ideas about education or learning
- The impact of fundamentally different interpersonal styles
- The importance of contrasting personal core beliefs

Mentees should regard such fundamental and possibly volatile problems as extending *beyond* the proper boundaries of the typical mentoring session.

Two Approaches to Resolving Conflict

In attempting to resolve a conflict, the mentee should consider the following two approaches before deciding to terminate the relationship:

1. Meet with the mentor to openly discuss the problem. Place special emphasis on determining if the mentor also agrees that there is a significant interpersonal or other issue, and is prepared to work it out in a joint effort.

2. Request an intervention by the administrator as an objective third party and try to arrive at an acceptable solution. This attempt may reveal an initial misunderstanding that can be resolved through the clarification of expectations or the willingness to modify previously held views.

As a cautionary note, if the mentor and mentee clash (whether subtly or dramatically) over differences between them, the mentee would be wise to remember that *early* indications of conflict should not be interpreted as a warning signal to instantly terminate the relationship. Such events may actually represent a very healthy opportunity to explore and understand—though not necessarily to adopt or to accept—other personality characteristics or viewpoints on issues.

Mentees should remain vigilant in ensuring they do not easily abandon their opportunity for learning. Clearly, other approaches can be explored, such as assignment to a different mentor or reentry into the program at a later time.

The Productive Use of Time: Understanding and Working within the Boundaries of Mentoring

The productive use of time is essential to the mentoring experience, and requires that both mentee and mentor understand, respect, and work within the boundaries of the mentoring process and the program's requirements. Misconceptions and inappropriate actions in this regard include the following:

▪ *Separately renegotiating the conditions of the original mentor–mentee agreement.* Mentees must realize that neither they nor their mentors are "authorized" to separately renegotiate the conditions of the agreement—accepted in good faith—for engaging in a mentoring program advocated by a sponsoring organization.

■ *Requesting or accepting a highly modified agenda.* It is inappropriate to request or to accept a diluted, improperly expanded, or otherwise highly modified agenda as a substitute for the learning experience of one-to-one mentoring. In most cases, such changes would be inconsistent with legitimate program objectives.

■ *Misinterpreting the concept of mentoring.* This problem may appear early on in the mentoring relationship, resulting in differing opinions about how to interpret program methods, activities, or objectives. Often, either the mentor, the mentee, or both did not fully comprehend the concept of mentoring as a workplace *learning* experience that was presented at early orientation meetings or in the subsequent explanations and readings. Fortunately, when the problem is identified, any related conflicts are usually resolvable after sufficient explanation.

It should be noted, however, that once the program's purpose and requirements are fully understood, if either the mentor or the mentee is unable to accept the guidelines essential to creating a successful mentoring experience, withdrawal from the program may be the most reasonable decision.

■ *Allowing personal or workplace problems to dominate the sessions.* Mentees must carefully weigh the consequences of using sessions to deal with personal or workplace problems. Even issues that are indirectly connected to meeting mentoring objectives but possibly capable of being worked out with mentors should *not* be given time more appropriately spent in promoting the mentee's self-development as an adult learner.

Serious problems (such as issues related to family, work performance, and personnel conflicts) certainly can and often do arise. But mentee and mentor alike must understand that these issues cannot always be addressed meaningfully *within* a mentor–mentee relationship without altering the basic purpose of the mentoring program. Dealing with complex emotional, psychological, or situational problems is the proper domain of qualified specialists, and mentees should expect that if such problems arise, mentors will refer them to professionals who can provide the time and help they need. The mentee has to be prepared to take the initiative, if necessary, and to request that the mentor recommend a specialist.

Above all, to make the most productive use of time, mentees must remain focused on their primary reason for entering into a mentoring relationship—career and professional development—and pursue topics and activities that are relevant to the mentoring dialogue and thus to the goals of the program.

Chapter 3

MAINTAINING A MENTEE JOURNAL

The Journal and Its Uses

Keeping a journal while involved in the mentoring process is a good way for mentees to take their self-development one step further toward goal achievement. The journal can serve a number of purposes but is best used as:

1. An accurate source of information for later reference

2. An ongoing register of ideas for learning activities and projects

In this chapter, we will take a closer look at both uses.

1. An Accurate Source of Information

Mentees can assume that at some point in the future they will get the chance to list successful participation in the mentoring program as an important career-related experience. Having a record of their participation in the form of accurate and reasonably comprehensive notes can support their goals for that future, especially if they are asked to supply an account of their experience on a résumé or to answer specific questions about it during a job interview.

Whether dealing with a potential employer or an evaluator in a competitive promotion situation, mentees will usually be asked to explain how mentoring contributed to employee learning and competency. Typically, the other parties try to determine the relevance of the experience to their own workplace environment, directly asking questions to elicit the unique perspective only the mentee can offer.

In such a situation, mentees enjoy a notable advantage if they have reviewed a journal containing reasonably substantial details of their experience beforehand. They can easily reconstruct a coherent portrait of their involvement and lend insight into how the benefits from one-to-one learning will transfer as skills into a different workplace context.

In contrast, mentees who lack the information resources of a journal will find it difficult to discuss their mentoring involvement in clear terms. Sometimes they may even appear unable to provide any insight into skills transferral. Obviously, mentees who can deliver only generalized and vague responses are apt to suffer diminished credibility, particularly in their assertion that the program resulted in significant professional development. Their account will be less than persuasive because it lacks appropriately detailed evidence.

For a numbers of reasons, then, mentees should be prepared to rely on their own records, even if the mentor is allowed to offer a letter of recommendation. Normally, a mentee's journal will be more factual than a mentor's notes, and more reflective of the specifics of individual learning.

2. An Ongoing Register of Ideas

A journal can also serve an important purpose during the evolving mentor–mentee relationship as an ongoing register of ideas for learning activities and projects.

By using a journal to create a continuing databank of learning proposals, mentees often discover that the very attempt to produce a pool of ideas is often a productive and stimulating personal experience. Entries regarding projects the mentee plans to explore can be included in the journal and then raised for discussion with the mentor at subsequent sessions.

Moreover, by reviewing the entries, mentees can better identify recurrent themes and interests and more precisely monitor their ongoing development of particular skills and proficiencies. Such a conscious review should be considered an important aspect of the mentees' responsibility for ensuring that their legitimate expectations for learning are being met.

As the mentoring relationship evolves, mentees will be in a better position to reflect objectively on the accumulating record of events, especially with regard to determining whether their original goals for the program are being achieved. If the situation warrants, mentees can then address their proper concerns to mentors in a more organized form.

Chapter 4

THE POLICY OF USING MENTORS AS REFERENCES

Preliminary Considerations

It is important to note that the policy of some programs is to discourage the use of mentors as references. Although initially this approach might seem a surprising limitation, mentees should weigh the advantages and disadvantages of the idea.

Even when there is no official prohibition against the practice, mentees themselves might benefit as adult learners if they choose *not* to request that mentors serve as a source for letters of recommendation. The decision will often depend on the ability of mentees to carefully distinguish between their primary and secondary reasons for participating in mentoring programs.

Reasons for the No-Use Policy

The rationale for the policy is to avoid putting mentors in the position of acting as formal evaluators of their mentees, a situation that could place unwarranted constraints on the mentees' ability to be honest with their mentors. The major concern is that if mentees become overly invested in cultivating their mentors as future candidates for references, some of them may develop an unproductive interest in promoting their own image as "self-idealized," nearly perfect employees.

The basic purpose of mentoring is to provide the participants with an opportunity to engage in meaningful dialogues and activities based on honest exchanges, *not* to create situations that offer mentees the possibility of relating to their mentors as only personnel to be impressed. Although not a frequent motive, some mentees might even view the situation as a chance for them to take unfair advantage of their mentors by attempting to cultivate their good will as a means of promoting a gold-plated future reference.

Obviously, such a manipulative agenda would contradict the unmistakable goal of mentoring: to encourage mentees to pursue the beneficial, solution-oriented approach of *sharing rather than camouflaging* their private uncertainties, and of openly exploring workable strategies to develop their career or academic competencies.

In this regard, it is worth mentioning that programs that assign managers as mentors to their own employees *must* directly question the wisdom of relying on recognized authority figures as workplace mentors. In these instances, mentees are put in the uncomfortable position of deciding whether they can place a high level of confidence in their mentors—those with whom they are asked to be "totally honest." This is an especially difficult situation because the same senior staff usually evaluate their mentees' professional proficiency and suitability for promotion.

Mentees must be prepared to demonstrate prudent judgment—and must conclude they are essentially "safe"—before they agree to disclose information to their mentor-managers that could create discomfort or uncertainty about their suitability for particular workplace assignments and responsibilities.

It is conceivable that even well-intentioned mentors will overreact to certain personal revelations by mentees. Whether the disclosure is directly connected to workplace competencies or not, they might prompt the mentor to form the unjustified opinion that the mentee is not the "right" person for a job or promotion. Mentees should certainly not become paranoid, but neither should they rush in too quickly; each mentee should carefully examine every mentoring situation on its own merits.

The Issue of Trust

The issue of trust as a significant problem can be overstated and is not always applicable to all situations or relationships. Mentees should not automatically assume that the self-disclosure of important perceptions and facts will always be seriously compromised because a reference might later be requested. However, mentees in a position to request references should consider whether *for them* having frank conversations with their mentors could result in negative consequences and therefore place the critical factor of "trust" at risk.

Reference Seeking as an Obstacle to Trust

To be genuinely meaningful, the mentoring relationship must be firmly anchored in open and honest dialogue. Consequently, the mentee should regard as relevant any factor, including letters of reference and formal evaluations, that might compromise the essential component of trust.

For example, let's take a further look at the major concern behind the no-use policy. Mentees who indeed (and mistakenly) value their mentors only as future references, and view the cultivation of self-image as serving their best interests, naturally avoid honest engagement in dialogue. They enter the mentoring process with a hidden agenda from which trust is necessarily excluded, and so are prepared to withhold information about needed self-improvements. From their perspective, the mention of any weakness, however minimal that weakness, could immediately jeopardize their chance to become candidates for advancement.

Such mentees, in preferring to remain in the secure zone of examining *just* their marketable strengths, not only undermine the proper goals of mentoring but also risk limiting, or completely missing, beneficial career or training opportunities. Thus it is actually in the mentee's best interest to also confront—and to disclose—the pressing need to pursue areas of development, even if they are associated with personal or professional discomfort and uncertainty.

A Word on Genuine Self-Disclosure

Of course, endeavors that call for genuine self-disclosure are not easily undertaken, and to effectively explore sensitive areas, particularly those that may be ego-threatening, a skilled mentor and a courageous mentee are required. A valuable agreement for both to honor is that the content of the sessions will remain *confidential* unless the parties mutually decide otherwise.

Mentees and mentors should, however, carefully consider what is appropriate self-disclosure in the context of the mentoring model of learning. Some thoughts or feelings are clearly unsuitable as topics. This issue should be directly raised and resolved early in the mentoring relationship.

Reference Policies and Mentee Decisions

If the program has a no-use policy, mentees should not immediately reject the program or consider it worthless. As we have seen above, there are some serious drawbacks to allowing references. Nonetheless, mentees may still want to consider whether the inability to request and receive a letter of recommendation could have a bearing on their future and possibly be construed as a negative comment on their work performance and competency.

If the program allows references, mentees need to review the total situation before planning to ask mentors for them. While there may be no negative impact on the sharing, collaboration, and learning so vital to the mentoring experience, the potential for harm does exist, and mentees should be aware of this and even raise it as a legitimate issue with their mentors (doing so *well before* requesting a letter of recommendation). Overall, the deciding factor in favor of using the mentor as a reference should be the mentee's well-founded certainty that such action will have no deleterious effect on the mentor–mentee relationship.

Chapter 5

UNDERSTANDING THE
COMPLETE MENTOR ROLE

The Mentor Role

The complete mentor role is based on a synthesis of mentoring behaviors that adult-education specialists consider essential for the development of meaningful mentor–mentee relationships. Its purpose is to provide mentors with a coherent framework and valid, reliable guidelines for maximizing their overall contribution to the career, training, and academic progress of mentees.

The model comprises six distinct categories of behavior (shown below), which together describe how mentors can meet two important goals:

1. Facilitating productive interactions in their evolving relationships with mentees

2. Integrating and balancing the components of the interpersonal relationship

By using the model as a reference point, mentors can come reasonably close to achieving the ideal characterized by the term *complete*.

The Complete Mentor Role Behavioral Categories

1. Relationship
2. Information
3. Facilitative
4. Confrontative
5. Mentor Model
6. Employee Vision

The Value of the Concept for Mentees

There are a number of reasons why it is important for mentees to understand the concept and apply it, including the following:

■ Their knowledge of the model, which they share with mentors, can improve their ability to interact with mentors as collaborative learners.

■ They gain insight into the theory and practice underlying their mentors' initiatives and reactions; as a result, they are more capable of relating as informed partners to the variety of opportunities offered to them.

■ As aware participants, mentees are in a better position to realistically assess the extent to which their mentors are fulfilling the duties of mentoring, including meeting the mentees' unique needs.

Equipped with this level of understanding, mentees can take constructive initiatives to ensure that the time spent with mentors is used fully and directed toward achieving their career, training, and educational goals.

Knowing and Doing—The Need for Application

It is certainly reasonable to expect that by gaining a more comprehensive view of the complex cluster of behaviors defined as the complete mentor role, employees will, from the start, be more responsive in their role as mentees.

However, while this form of preparation for the mentoring program should enhance the learning curve, mentees cannot assume that knowledge alone will automatically result in significant action. Mentees must also be prepared to *apply* that knowledge, particularly by:

■ Diligently creating and responding to professional and educational development activities

■ Continually engaging in the process and attempting to interact as strongly committed learners

Self-Advocates, Not Imitators

The explanation of mentor behaviors is not intended to suggest that mentees mechanically respond as mirror images of their mentors, nor is it meant to imply that the mentee must always react with a set of behaviors that correspond to, or mimic, those of the mentor. The essential point is that when mentees are familiar with the strategies and behaviors typical of mentors, they are more apt to respond as intelligent and skillful adult learners.

As self-advocates, the more mentees can help mentors meet their responsibilities in all the dimensions of mentoring interaction, the more likely the chance that mentees will benefit from the advantages of the one-to-one model of learning. The astute mentee would be wise—as a partner with a vested interest in the outcome of the program—to understand the mentor role and contribute to its successful realization.

The Six Dimensions of the Mentor Role

The Dimensions and Corresponding Mentee Behavior

Figure 1, on the following page, shows the six dimensions of mentor behavior along with their key points and characteristics. Also shown is a correlated behavioral profile of the mentee as a collaborative adult learner, suggesting the basic components of the complete *mentee* role.

Emphases and Preparation for Mentors and Mentees

Generally, sponsored programs encourage mentors to accept the model's behavioral guidelines and, in doing so, emphasize these necessities:

▪ Recognizing the relevance of all six behavioral dimensions and the mentor's contribution to the overall meaning of the mentoring experience

▪ Properly attuning themselves to the importance of performing at a productive level of proficiency in each behavioral dimension

Most programs ensure that mentors understand the purpose of the guidelines: to facilitate significant learning and attainment of the goals of one-to-one education. As a result of such preparation, mentors are better able to assume their share of the accountability for the ultimate value of the mentoring relationship as a learning opportunity.

In this respect, mentees, too, require (and usually receive) encouragement and preparation. After all, the venture cannot succeed if mentees do not accept

FIGURE 1   Behavioral Profile of an Effective Mentee

MENTOR BEHAVIORS

1. RELATIONSHIP
   Key Point — Trust

   ▮ Shares and reflects on experiences
   ▮ Listens empathetically
   ▮ Understands and accepts

2. INFORMATION
   Key Point — Advice

   ▮ Offers facts about career, education,
     plans, progress
   ▮ Comments about use of information
   ▮ Exhibits tailored, accurate,
     and sufficient knowledge

3. FACILITATIVE
   Key Point — Alternatives

   ▮ Explores interests, abilities, ideas, beliefs
   ▮ Provides other views/attainable goals
   ▮ Shares personal decisions about career,
     training, education

4. CONFRONTATIVE
   Key Point — Challenge

   ▮ Shows respect for decisions, actions, career
   ▮ Shares insight into counterproductive
     strategies and behaviors
   ▮ Evaluates need and capacity to change

5. MENTOR MODEL
   Key Point — Motivation

   ▮ Discloses life experience as role model
   ▮ Personalizes and enriches relationship
   ▮ Takes risks; Overcomes difficulties in
     education and career

6. EMPLOYEE VISION
   Key Point — Initiative

   ▮ Thinks critically about career future
   ▮ Considers personal/professional potential
   ▮ Initiates change; Negotiates transitions

MENTEE BEHAVIORS

▮ Offers Detailed Explanations
▮ Expects Mentor to Listen
  and to Ask Questions

▮ Provides Facts and Records
▮ Expects Mentor to Review
  Use and Depth of Sources

▮ Explains Choices and Decisions
▮ Expects Mentor to Pose
  Options and Other Views

▮ Reflects on Initiatives
▮ Expects Mentor to Examine
  Goals and Approach

▮ Expresses Main Concerns
▮ Expects Mentor to Share
  Ideas and Feelings

▮ Visualizes Own Future
▮ Expects Mentor to Examine
  Plans and Encourage Progress

their share of equivalent responsibility and respond with behaviors that foster the mentor–mentee relationship. The profile shown in Figure 1 gives mentees the behavioral model they need for relevant participation. Its guidelines, in correlating with those of the mentor's role, prepare them for and effectively support the one-to-one model of learning.

Chapter 6

THE PHASES OF MENTORING

Significance for Mentees

The six dimensions of the complete mentor role are viewed as a set of highly significant and distinct mentoring behaviors. We can add value to the mentor model if we expand that perspective and also view its six dimensions within the context of the evolving mentoring experience. In doing so, we find that their order *generally* parallels the developmental progression—or phases—of that experience. We see as well that the phases of mentoring tend to occur in a logical pattern, with reasonably clear continuity throughout the duration of mentor–mentee contact.

Correlation of Phases, Dimensions, and Key Points

Phases	Dimensions	Key Points
Early	Relationship	Trust
Middle	Information	Advice
Later	Facilitative Confrontative	Alternatives Challenge
Final	Mentor Model Mentee Vision	Motivation Initiative

An illustration of this perspective, with the correlation of the phases, six dimensions, and key points of mentoring behavior, is shown below.

Mentees need to incorporate this expanded viewpoint of phases and dimensions into their knowledge of mentoring for four important reasons:

1. In recognizing the complete mentor role as a synergistic approach to the interpersonal dynamics of the six dimensions, mentees will find a framework for understanding the overall purpose of the mentoring model of learning.

2. The viewpoint will heighten the mental alertness required to respond meaningfully to, and benefit from, the cognitive, psychological, and affective connections between the mentoring phases and the dimensions and key points of the complete mentor role.

3. Mentees will be aware that the ongoing face-to-face dialogue and activity that occur within particular mentor–mentee sessions may *not* always follow the order of dimensions or phases as smoothly or neatly as expected.

4. Mentees will understand that the mentor's ability to help the mentee is usually demonstrated by reasonable control of the process of one-to-one development as it changes over time; consequently, they should not perceive the mentor's actions as unanticipated or random attempts to offer assistance (and can offer constructive feedback if necessary about any concerns).

The Need for Flexibility

Mentees should approach the above construct of the complete mentor role by relying on this critical guideline:

> The mentoring model will *not* always represent the specific type of dialogue or activity that transpires in the mentoring session; *neither* will it always predict at exactly what point a particular event of significant learning will occur along the continuum suggested by the six mentoring dimensions.

This guideline points to the need for flexibility in the application of the mentoring approach. Mentees should use the model as a means of understanding the importance of each mentor dimension as a component of what, for the mentee, will essentially be a *holistic* experience, especially as the mentor–mentee relationship unfolds over time.

Indeed, in reflecting on the final value of that experience, mentees often interpret the underlying framework of dimensions and phases as an overall learning event that occurred in a particular time frame; they do not necessarily interpret it analytically, as a series of highly charged insights associated with a particular dimension or phase.

For mentees, a flexible application is useful because it captures the full potential inherent in the mentoring experience—including the significance of the mentee role—without suggesting that mentors are not vital influences on the dynamics of one-to-one interaction and, thus, on the degree of learning derived from ongoing mentor–mentee contact.

Shift in Responsibility

In a genuine sense, the word *complete* is intended to convey that the mentor's positive influence on a mentee occurs primarily as a result of the mentor's achieving a productive balance of the six separate dimensions—in essence, that the synergistic combination and application of mentoring skills facilitates a successful learning experience. This intended meaning is essential to our understanding of the mentor model, but we must recognize as well that the word *complete* also directly recommends the proactive involvement of the mentee.

In the original model of mentoring, the emphasis that education specialists placed on responsibility was somewhat weighted on the side of mentor responsibility for constructive outcomes. The mentee was considered a beneficiary responsible for meaningful involvement, but more in the sense of being a reasonable co-participant who had less direct authority or accountability for positive results.

The Mentee's Guide clearly, and legitimately, tilts the idea of responsible participation more toward mentees by requesting their informed, serious initiatives and responses in *all* the dimensions and phases of mentoring. The major point is not that the mentor is less accountable than before; rather, that the emphasis has shifted toward the relevance of the informed and active mentee as a positive influence *on the mentor*, and thus on the final worth of the commitment both have made to achieve a collaborative mentor–mentee experience of lasting value.

If mentees use the idea of the dimensions and phases as a *guide* for traveling through one-to-one interaction—and not as a fixed map in which every step is expected to be marked or every path assumed to be linked mechanically to another—then they will properly enter into mentoring as a developmental process of learning.

Chapter 7

MENTEE RESPONSES TO MENTORING BEHAVIOR

Introduction

In this chapter, we will take a closer look at the six behavioral dimensions of the complete mentor model. The material will provide the mentee with the following:

1. A background explanation of each behavioral dimension's purpose, definition, and key point, along with a list of related mentor behaviors

2. Guidance that promotes effective *mentee* responses and actions

Dimension 1—Relationship

Essential Purpose

The mentor creates a psychological climate of trust, which allows the mentee (who understands the mentor is listening, not judging) to honestly share and reflect on his or her positive and negative experiences in the workplace.

Core Definition

The mentor conveys a genuine understanding and acceptance of the mentee's feelings through active, empathetic listening.

Mentor Behaviors

- Practice responsive listening (verbal and nonverbal behaviors that signal sincere interest).

- Ask open-ended questions related to the mentee's expressed immediate concerns about actual situations.

- Provide descriptive feedback based on observations rather than inferences of motives.

- Use perception checks to ensure comprehension of the mentee's feelings.

- Offer nonjudgmental, sensitive responses that help clarify emotional states and reactions.

Key Point—TRUST

The centerpiece of relationship behavior is the creation of trust between mentor and mentee. In fact, the term *relationship* is repeatedly used in various ways—with trust embedded in the core meaning—to describe the general interpersonal interaction between mentor and mentee.

Underlying Structure

The relationship dimension is the underlying structure on which the entire mentoring transaction is based, and on which mentor and mentee will depend to maximize the potential for extending into the other five categories of mentoring behaviors. Any mentor who attempts to fulfill the responsibilities of the complete mentor role will first need to establish relationship as the foundation of mentoring dialogue.

Mentees therefore should recognize the importance of trust as the factor that allows them to understand and accept that the mentor's ideas, views, and advice are offered in good faith.

Perception of Trust

The bond of trust—the belief that the mentor is acting in the best interests of the mentee—is the *cornerstone* of the successful mentor–mentee relationship. It supports the mentee's ability to fully engage the mentor as a partner in genuinely collaborative dialogue, spend time considering the mentor's viewpoints, make informed decisions, and take action as an independent adult learner.

Without trust, the facts, records, research, analysis, and guidance that should be meaningful components of one-to-one interaction will have limited value, because the mentee will likely discount the worth of the information, considering it of little direct and personal significance. Not surprisingly, advice from a mentor in whom the mentee has low confidence will usually fail to generate the motivation needed to act on that advice. Also, the mentor's interpretation of "facts," when different from the mentee's, will be dismissed in spite of their potential value.

The Mentor's Role in Establishing Trust

Mentees should expect that mentors will try to communicate they are trustworthy persons in whom mentees can place their confidence within the proper boundaries of the mentoring model. Certainly, this mutual understanding would include the recognition that their exchange of viewpoints will primarily center on areas relevant to work-related issues and topics.

The simple truism "Why take seriously the advice of a person who appears not to really care about you?" is a powerful reality. To deal with this mentee concern, mentors are instructed to pay direct attention to establishing trust as a critical element of face-to-face learning. Much of the verbal and nonverbal behavior displayed by mentors will thus be a sincere and necessary—though not manipulative—effort to promote the "trust connection" between themselves and their mentees.

Rational Involvement

Although mentees need not rush headlong into placing absolute trust in mentors, they should enter into mentoring with the reasonable assumption that mentors are properly concerned about their career and professional development.

The willingness of mentees to invest themselves rationally and honestly in the initial mentoring dialogue is significant because trust, as a vital component in healthy, normal interaction, is not usually the result of accelerated attempts to establish a warm, accepting, and nonjudgmental interpersonal climate; rather, trust develops from the gradual, often subtle but always definite, incremental phases of mutual involvement.

From the very first session, mentees can contribute to the acceleration of the learning curve by accepting mentors as operating in good faith. If mentees are more consumed with second-guessing their mentors' motives for participating in the program, then the time and energy that should be devoted to the goals of mentoring can easily be diverted into unproductive areas.

Assumption of Trust

Mentees would be wise to grant their mentors the initial respect of *assuming* mentors are trustworthy and sincere in purpose. This means the mentee must accept two propositions:

- That mentors are not on trial to prove their good intentions

- That the expected integrity of mentors is an appropriate entry-point expectation for the mentoring experience

Although subsequent involvement with the mentor may provide evidence to the contrary—and suggest that the immediate granting of trust was an unwise decision—mentees will discover that such a negative development is the clear exception and not the general rule.

In approaching the assumption of trust, mentees need to remember these important points:

- Mentees should never feel compelled to provide personally sensitive information, or to engage in self-disclosure that could put them in a vulnerable position, before they have sufficient confidence or reason to do so. Some degree of substantive dialogue must take place prior to the creation of a reasonable mentee comfort zone.

- Operating as if a baseline of trust already exists simply because it would be an ideal pier from which to launch a meaningful interpersonal relationship is not what is meant by the advice that mentees should initially be trusting. The purpose of trust must be viewed in the context of the proper roles of mentor and mentee and the objectives of one-to-one education.

- One of the mentee's goals is to fit the profile of the receptive, prudently honest, and fully involved adult learner, capable of participating in mature mentoring interaction. This profile differs significantly from that of a mentee who is confused, naive, imposes unjustified expectations on the mentor, or cannot comprehend why some types of self-revelation are clearly inappropriate.

Mutual trust is a healthy reference point for entry into a wide range of topics that are consistent with the anticipated content and concerns of mentoring. With trust as the interpersonal cornerstone, the mentor and mentee can cross into many relevant developmental areas of learning that require secure balance, proper timing, and sensitive actions and reactions.

Dimension 2—Information

Essential Purpose

The mentor ensures that "tailored" advice is based on accurate and sufficient knowledge of individual mentees.

Core Definition

The mentor directly requests detailed facts from the mentee regarding his or her current plans for and progress in achieving career, training, and educational goals. The mentor also offers specific comments regarding the relevance of sources and the usefulness of information.

Mentor Behaviors

- Ask questions aimed at ensuring factual understanding of present job and career situation.

- Review relevant background to develop adequate work-related personal profile.

- Ask probing questions that require concrete answers.

- Offer directive-type comments about present problems and solutions that should be considered.

- Make restatements to ensure factual accuracy and clarity of interpretive understanding.

- Rely on facts as an integral component of decision making.

Key Point—ADVICE

Mentees should consider advice to be most valuable when it is specific rather than general. Mentors are even instructed to be explicit when they are only "thinking out loud," so that mentees do not interpret obvious or off-the-cuff answers as literal advice.

Such a cautious approach is not intended to muzzle normal, spontaneous dialogue, but rather to help mentors avoid these dangers:

- The possibility that general or casual comments will be confused with substantive, mentee-specific recommendations. Although not the usual scenario, inexperienced mentees sometimes do quietly act on, rather than question, remarks that are so vague as to mean "all things to all people."

- The possibility that mentees will come to view the mentor's comments as symptomatic of a patronizing or unconcerned attitude. When mentees believe the mentor is condescending to them or does not care, the very foundation of the mentor–mentee relationship can be put at risk or sorely undermined.

Mentor Responsibility and the Need for Mentee Feedback

Mentees should find that in most situations mentors are careful not to create the impression they are offering serious responses to important questions when they are only relating more casually to the mentee's particular situation. However, mentees must be aware that even well-meaning mentors can occasionally slip into the trap of offering quick advice that, lacking careful consideration, provides little more than nonspecific, fill-in-the-blank type of remarks. In such cases, mentees should directly ask questions about their interpretation of the mentor's comments, regardless of how obvious the answers may seem.

As a group, mentors are very aware of their responsibility as advisors. They realize that generalized advice can divert discussion away from the mentee's particular concerns, and that facile remarks can confuse, mislead, and discourage mentees. Moreover, mentors have a *vested interest* in helping mentees approach specific issues as thoughtful adult learners. In light of these facts, mentees should never feel reluctant to raise their concerns about the course a discussion is taking, or to inquire about the type of advice a mentor is offering. Of course, if the mentee unsuccessfully follows the advice, or believes it is so vague that practical implementation is unfeasible, the mentee *must* directly raise his or her concerns with the mentor. Usually mentors will acknowledge there is indeed a problem after it is pointed out to them.

Although mentees should not expect the mentor's every word to be filled with golden meaning, they should view frequent abstract and generalized mentor guidance as better left unspoken. A mentor who has unwittingly strayed down this unproductive road will benefit from—and as a professional should be prepared to hear—polite feedback in the form of a reality check offered in good faith by the mentee. Yet, mentees must also remember that there are many reasons why the good intentions of mentors sometimes backfire—most of which have little to do with personal motive. Again, when in doubt, mentees should not assume; they should inquire. The essential first step toward remedying a problem is for the mentee to request guidance directly.

Seek Tailored Advice

The word *tailored* suggests a situation in which the proper fit occurs because of personal attention to detail, as exemplified by hands-on, time intensive, face-to-face interaction—the result of genuine dialogue between mentor and mentee. In this respect, "off-the-rack" information will not usually accommodate the *unique* needs of the mentee.

Mentoring is clearly about the acquisition, interpretation, and application of information for the purpose of promoting the career and educational development of mentees. Quite naturally, mentors are typically prepared to expend energy on topics and activities directly connected to the *specific* learning goals of mentoring programs. Many of them understand that time spent with the mentee to enhance individual growth *is* the essential task of the complete mentor.

From the informed mentee's perspective, then, the increased "time on task" that tailoring requires is entirely appropriate. Only by the mutual devotion of their time can mentor and mentee work together to properly fit and adjust the details essential to assessing, planning, and fulfilling the mentee's goals.

A Detailed Mentee Picture

What mentees can contribute to the collaborative process is their active participation as partners in the sharing and analysis of relevant facts. By offering concrete information about their backgrounds, goals, and plans, mentees can provide the mentor with the opportunity to respond based on a clear picture of the mentee as a unique individual.

For the mentor, the immediate advantage of having a more detailed portrait is the enhanced ability to engage in dialogue and activities directly connected to the mentee's learning objectives. Obviously, the more quickly and accurately mentees can have their agendas addressed, the more likely the chance that the one-to-one relationship will help fulfill their expectations as a meaningful growth experience.

Eliciting the Facts—Interpersonal Style

At times it may seem that the mentor is rather insistent on collecting information. Some mentors may appear so obsessed with this task that the mentee begins to wonder if the barrage of questions will ever end. In extreme situations, the mentee might even feel as if the proverbial and unpleasant "third degree" grilling session is underway.

In other cases, the mentor may use a more indirect approach to eliciting information. Mentees who are immediately ready to engage in substantive dialogue could find this gradual style of inquiry unnecessarily slow. As a consequence, they might feel the need to assert themselves and even boldly announce they would rather just "get to the point."

Mentees who have particular preferences about the pace of the process, especially with regard to the mentor's style of collecting and providing information, should share their views with mentors.

Mentees should also be aware that many mentors will overtly attempt to elicit from them *adequately* detailed and precise explanations about important issues and concerns. Several helpful techniques (advocated in books and taught in training sessions) that mentors are encouraged to use include:

- Probing—Directly asking the mentee highly precise questions that require concrete and specific answers

- Restating—Paraphrasing (summarizing) the mentee's statements as a means of ensuring they have correctly understood the mentee's ideas and attitudes

- Perception checking—Sharing their viewpoint of what the mentee believes or feels about the subject under discussion, to determine if their interpretation is an accurate reflection of the mentee's real meaning

When mentees realize that such attempts are legitimate efforts to collect solid data (build a factual/cognitive profile) and to understand the real person behind the data (build an emotional/psychological profile), they are better able to cooperate with the approach. Also, it is important for mentees to be flexible and to make allowances for their mentors if the latter are not masters of the interpersonal skills needed to implement the method to the complete satisfaction of *all* mentees.

Mentee Preparation of Facts

From the very first session, mentees should be prepared to provide a complete factual profile of themselves. Records and summaries of academic, training, and workplace history should be made available, along with any additional material that could give the mentor a more coherent picture of their prior and current endeavors.

In many cases, the mentee will be asked to complete a mentee-profile form, which should be filled out as soon as possible. (If a profile form is not made available, the mentee should offer to provide this data at the earliest opportunity.) Usually the mentee will be asked to explain such points as:

1. Career goals—Provide a personal statement about professional goals and reasons for decisions.

2. Educational objectives—Identify degrees, certification, colleges, major field of concentration.

3. Training plans—Specify workshops, seminars, internships, job rotations, special projects.

4. Strategies for achieving goals—Clarify specific ideas for placing and maintaining oneself in positive positions.

5. Present actions—Explain current activities to advance progress.

6. Available resources—Provide comments about status of support from family, friends, workplace staff.

7. Concerns—Clarify issues about finances, time, energy, aptitudes, skills, abilities, interests, other personal or social responsibilities.

Again, cooperation is essential. If mentees supply solid facts on profile forms, and provide further information as needed, then mentors can build a reliable database for giving *genuine* advice—the kind that truly and significantly addresses the *specific* concerns of each mentee.

In regard to the information dimension, then, both mentor and mentee should consider this phase of interaction as important not only for building a reasonably comfortable climate that promotes continuing dialogue, but also for creating an accurately and sufficiently detailed portrait of the mentee as a unique individual.

Dimension 3—Facilitative

Essential Purpose

The mentor helps the mentee consider alternative views while reaching his or her own decisions about attainable career, training, and educational objectives.

Core Definition

The mentor guides the mentee through a reasonably indepth review and exploration of his or her interests, abilities, ideas, and beliefs revelant to the workplace.

Mentor Behaviors

- Pose hypothetical questions to expand individual views.

- Uncover underlying experiential and informational bases for assumptions.

- Present multiple viewpoints to generate more indepth analysis of decisions and options.

- Examine the seriousness of the mentee's commitment to achieving personal goals.

- Analyze reasons for current pursuits.

- Review specific work-related preferences and career interests.

Key Point—ALTERNATIVES

Mentees should approach the exploration of alternatives as a four-step process. The mentor will do the following (although not always in this exact order):

1. Review the mentee's present and future career, training, and educational objectives.

2. Identify the ideas and beliefs underlying the mentee's choice of objectives.

3. Clarify the approaches selected by the mentee to achieve success, as demonstrated by such specific endeavors as plans, strategies, decisions, solutions, and actions.

4. Propose different viewpoints and other options (as needed) that offer professional and academic pathways for the mentee to consider and possibly explore.

Mentees, then, should see the mentor's review as an analysis primarily conducted to understand three elements:

- The mentee's goals

- The reasoning and influences behind the mentee's choice of goals

- The tangible efforts the mentee has made toward meeting the goals

Mentor as Reality Check

In examining these elements, the mentor basically functions as a reality check whose principal role is to uncover the bedrock of sources—thoughts, experiences (indirect as well as direct), factual information, and conclusions—that mentees have relied on to form their views and to guide their decisions.

Mentees should understand that the ultimate purpose of the mentor's questions is not to extract justifications for their choices; rather, it is to help mentees examine their sources' quality and worth (accuracy, reliability, completeness, relevance), with special emphasis on how they have interpreted the data in terms of personal lifestyle and career choices. The real value of the review is the extent to which it illuminates the mentees' *application* of opinions, facts, and experiences to their unique situations.

In such reviews, factors that might have had a subtle influence on mentees' perception of the workplace, such as ideas and beliefs shared with family and friends, will also be considered in addition to more obvious, work-related factors (such as the possible impact of managers and peers).

Of course, mentees who firmly believe they have made wise choices will see the review as an unnecessary task, and thus be reluctant to devote time and energy to it. Mentees who view themselves as clear, focused, and committed to handling the demands created by their own choices should certainly communicate this point to their mentors.

Advantages of Abbreviated Review

In cases where the mentor agrees with the mentee that a time-consuming and elaborate review may not be warranted, the mentor is likely to suggest using a compressed version rather than completely dismissing the topic. The mentee, rather than adamantly refusing to participate, should consider that this scaled-down approach offers two advantages:

1. The results of such an analysis could quickly confirm that the mentee is indeed pursuing goals based on substantive and detailed information.

2. The mentee's answers could reveal that he or she possesses a mature appraisal of the abilities and resources required to achieve the objectives.

Mentees should be receptive to the idea that *if* they are able to express thoughtful explanations that clarify the basic connections among their interests, aptitudes, and professional ambitions, then their self-confidence will be a well-founded and deserved asset.

Real versus Imagined

Mentees should also reflect on this easily overlooked fact: the mentee's ability to convey his or her viewpoint clearly, and to offer direct explanations for the selection of professional or academic credentials, is *no guarantee* that such choices are truly in the mentee's best interest. Even the most eloquently expressed, logical viewpoint can lack a core of wisdom.

Moreover, logic that is tidy and rehearsed can actually serve as a convenient smokescreen to shield the mentee from emotional discomfort; when such logic goes unchallenged, the mentee (whether knowingly or not) avoids the cognitive reflection essential to goal attainment and inherent in rigorous mentor–mentee dialogue. He or she may be able to visualize achieved objectives and satisfying rewards but unable to *directly* address the time, energy, and commitment demanded by their pursuit. This problem can be particularly acute if the mentee has never been required to confront the hard details of real-world success, but instead allowed to engage in vague fantasies and speculation about the pleasures awaiting in some magical realm of success.

Referral

The Need for Referral

The review process can sometimes force to the surface internal mentee conflicts, such as serious concerns or reservations about personal decisions. If this happens, both mentor and mentee would be prudent to consider referral to specialized helping professionals. Mentees should, in fact, *expect* the mentor to suggest referral if they are struggling with deep-seated, unresolved issues. Obviously, mentees who recognize there is a problem, and then accept the mentor's suggestion, can feel assured they are on the proper path toward a solution.

Mentees who decide to raise the issue of referral will be wise to keep these points in mind:

■ Interpersonal exchanges in which such sensitive topics are openly discussed will often be uncomfortable for both mentor and mentee. Mentees should therefore be prepared for taking this productive and mature step toward resolution, rather than approach it naively.

■ In acknowledging their willingness to accept help, mentees need to be very definite about their preference for referral to trained experts. Even well-meaning mentors who offer to work with them in the role of therapist must be viewed as stepping beyond the boundaries of the mentoring relationship.

It is also important for mentees to realize that if referral is raised as an option it does not mean the mentors will or should automatically try to handle the problem if they decline the offer.

Exploring Problems within the Mentoring Model

Of course, there will be some complicated problems that mentees can explore and possibly resolve *within* the mentoring model. For example, some mentees may already know that the motivation driving their decisions is the need to satisfy the ego (prove something to themselves) or to justify themselves to others. What they are legitimately seeking from the mentor is practical assistance with handling a recognized, well-defined problem.

Aware mentees who are eager to participate in self-analytical dialogue should remember that even conversations in which they willingly reevaluate personal decisions can prove to be quite difficult. For mentees with a *pronounced* personal as well as social ego-investment in achieving success in previously chosen areas, this type of self-examination could disappoint or even provoke disapproval from others who are heavily invested in the mentees' original decisions.

Mentees should therefore anticipate that the reconsideration process may sometimes be extremely stressful, especially if fueled by powerful factors such as the fixed expectations of workplace peers, managers, family, and friends, or if driven by the mentees' belief that only certain careers are socially respected and thus worthy of serious consideration.

The Mentor's Facilitative Role

Mentees who are determined to confront and to resolve a well-defined issue should certainly expect their mentors to serve as a reasonable source of advice, feedback, and support. Because the mentee's primary concern is not *why* there is a problem, but *how to deal* with a problem (especially if the mentee has definitely decided to change career or educational goals), mentors will usually consider the issue an appropriate subject for mentoring dialogue.

Thus, to take full advantage of the facilitative dimension of mentoring, mentees must be prepared to do the following:

■ Engage in a substantive review of relevant issues, choices, and options. This requires keeping an open mind. The mentee who appears overly vested in being "right" about his or her decisions should not be surprised if the mentor carefully points out that a clear refusal to review *any* choices, or to consider *other* reasonable options, signals that the mentee is no longer capable of questioning fixed pathways.

■ Participate in mutual appraisal of their personal approach to problem solving. Again, a candid inquiry is essential.

Mentees should welcome the opportunity to reexamine their commitment to a particular career or academic route. In this way, they can ensure it is based on a fully informed and personally significant assessment of the current and predicted future demands of a rapidly changing environment.

Review of Objectives

Mentees who have not yet formed definite views of their career, training, or educational objectives, or who are uncertain about their choices, should be ready to explore the unavoidable demands as well as the personal satisfaction and professional benefits experienced by people who have met their goals.

In short, mentees can usually expect to discuss with their mentors the step-by-step details of the journey, the overall map of the territory they will travel, and even the anticipated results of their arrival at the final destination. Of course, the longer-range implications of mentee decisions will be more difficult to assess meaningfully.

Resources to Meet Demands of the Journey

Mentors normally inquire about the variety of resources mentees need to complete their journey. General topics such as time, energy, and economics are translated into highly specific terms, as exemplified by the following questions.

1. Of the total quantity of time available, how much can be allocated to each particular endeavor?

2. What exact schedule is planned to handle daily activities and responsibilities?

3. Are there any anticipated future commitments that will seriously disrupt the planned schedule?

4. To what extent can work and lifestyle schedules be negotiated with other people?

5. Are there likely or even predictable situations at work or home which will require direct, personal attention?

6. Will outside financial and human resources (family, friends, institutions) be expected to provide assistance?

7. What is the extended time frame required to complete current goals?

8. Are there any issues that already appear to be real obstacles?

9. What problems, decisions, and strategies are, or need to be, immediately considered?

This list is not intended to patronize mentees by reducing the complex topic of resources to only nine questions; rather, it is meant to elucidate honest, basic concerns that require detailed answers. Mentees should expect the mentor (1) to view their ability to provide those answers as a key indicator of their commitment to participate in serious planning for the practical pursuit and attainment of goals, and (2) to engage them in a reasonably rigorous examination of the resources they are counting on to support their endeavors.

Dimension 4—Confrontative

Essential Purpose

The mentor helps the mentee gain insight into unproductive or counterproductive strategies or behaviors and helps the mentee evaluate his or her need and capacity to change.

Core Definition

The mentor respectfully challenges the mentee's explanations for or avoidance of decisions and actions relevant to his or her career development.

Mentor Behaviors

- Use careful probing to assess psychological readiness to benefit from different points of view.

- Make open acknowledgment of concerns about possible negative consequences of constructive criticism on relationship.

- Employ a confrontative verbal stance aimed at promoting self-assessment of discrepancies among career goals and commitment, strategies, and actions to achieve objectives.

- Select most likely behaviors and strategies for meaningful change.

- Use the least amount of carefully stated constructive criticism necessary for impact.

- Offer comments (before and after confrontational remarks) to reinforce belief in positive potential for growth beyond current situation.

Key Point—CHALLENGE

Because the term *confrontation* is often used to describe a hostile face-to-face situation, mentors and mentees must be absolutely clear about the meaning as applied to mentoring behavior. Here the word's usage, in all forms, is intended to emphasize the *challenge* so important for mentors to bring to the mentor–mentee dialogue; *it is not meant to suggest threat, intimidation, or any other harmful behavior*. This understanding is essential to fully comprehending the purpose of confrontative conduct.

Securing the Benefits of the Confrontative

Both mentor and mentee must understand the value as well as the risks (emotional as well as defensive) of relying on this approach as a constructive avenue for problem solving. To ensure that those benefits far outweigh the costs, the following precautionary measures should be taken:

1. At the start of their relationship, the mentor and mentee should address the topic of confrontive dialogue and the normal interpersonal tensions associated with it.

2. The mentee *recognizes* the benefits and thus enters the process attuned to the often difficult but highly valuable experience of confrontational interaction.

1. Confrontive Dialogue. Most mentors and mentees should be receptive to the value of engaging in confrontive dialogue if they acknowledge the difficulties and then focus on three important concerns:

- To reflect on and examine the way the mentor and the mentee, respectively, handle the interpersonal tension normally created by confrontation

- To underscore the necessity of applying effective behavioral skills to interpersonal relationships

- To avoid relying on "good intentions" alone to support the weight of interpersonal tension

It particularly important to clarify here that good intentions are in themselves insufficient for sending and receiving the types of complex messages that must inform the mentor–mentee relationship. Anyone with a firmly held idea to the contrary should not be viewed as merely naive about consequences; for adults, this attitude is usually a sign of immaturity about the necessity of accepting shared responsibility for, and applying behavioral skills to, interpersonal relationships.

2. Recognizing the Benefits. Mentees must be especially attuned to the primary value of the confrontative dimension. The challenging dialogue that marks this dimension is usually an extension of the critical task of the facilitative dimension, which is aimed at reviewing the factual connection among mentee potential, career and professional choices, and alternative viewpoints and action options.

Mentees should regard the confrontative dialogue as a step beyond the facilitative dialogue. It is more of an exacting appraisal about probable achievement, with its considerations based on a combination of factors, such as mentee aptitude, maturity, motivation, and applied problem-solving skills.

While mentors will base the dialogue on a realistic assessment of what the mentee seems capable of achieving in terms of stated goals, their particular emphasis will be on appraising *how* the mentee is attempting to ensure progress in the chosen field. Mentees should expect mentors to examine *collaboratively* and *directly* the extent to which mentees are successfully utilizing effective strategies to address current problems and prevent future ones.

Mentee Awareness of Constructive Behaviors

Because confrontative interaction is inherently a matter of posing direct questions and probing for detailed answers—that is, of creating constructive dialogue—the interpersonal process can sometimes seem intellectually rigorous. However, mentors are clearly instructed to avoid assuming the behavioral posture of a prosecuting attorney.

Legitimate assistance from the mentor is characterized by two-way, productive, assertive dialogue behaviors. To ensure that the dialogue is constructive and remains so, mentees should be aware of the impropriety of the following:

- *An argumentative verbal stance.* The discussion should be conducted in a reasonably calm and noncombative manner. Remember: the participants are not trying to win an argument; they are trying to analyze problems and arrive at workable solutions that will best serve the interests of the mentee.

- *An aggressive manner.* Mentors who display one-way domineering behaviors have crossed the proper boundaries of mentoring. When dealing with such a problem, mentees must share their concerns with the mentor in an appropriate manner and ensure that the importance of this issue is not mis-understood or minimized.

∎ *Sarcasm or ridicule.* It is highly unlikely the mentor's behavior will deterio-rate to such a degree, but if the improbable happens, the mentor should definitely voice his or her concerns.

It is essential that mentees who interpret the mentor's behavior as improper or discomforting respond with direct but respectful feedback. In this way, the mentor will know there is an issue at hand and have the opportunity to address it.

Mentees should be aware of their own behaviors, too, particularly with regard to defensiveness. They should be ready for the mentor's attempts to focus reflection on their *unhelpful* passive or active contributions to problems. This includes the possibility the mentor will raise concerns about their continuing inability to handle or resolve the difficult situations or issues confronting them. Naturally, most mentees will feel defensive to some degree during the initial phase of this approach. With preparation, though, mentees should be able to keep that degree to a minimum and to trust that the benefits of the approach will be worth any present discomfort.

Essential Value

Mentees should realize that the confrontative dimension, notably the review of their role as contributors to problems, is not based on the assumption that people have complete control over all the variables that influence their par-ticular choices, actions, or outcomes; rather, it is based on the practical knowl-edge that problem solving and goal attainment require a clear understanding of the factors people *can* control and an honest receptivity to making needed changes.

The review, then, is valuable as a way of helping mentees deal with obstacles to their goals by:

1. Identifying and understanding prior or current ineffectual behavioral pat-terns

2. Using the resultant insight to determine what actions might be implement-ed to produce realistic changes

3. Initiating practical solutions that produce positive results

4. Accepting cognitive feedback and emotional support during the experience

This facet of mentoring may not be simple or easy to engage in, but when it is successful, mentees receive truly significant assistance. Of course, when unsuccessful, it can jeopardize the ongoing mentor–mentee relationship as a valuable learning opportunity. Fortunately, the possibility of such failure is greatly reduced if both mentor and mentee enter into the confrontative dimension as informed and respectful collaborators on behalf of the mentee's development.

Confrontation Is Not Therapy

It is also important for mentees to recognize that the mentor is not attempting to conduct a "therapeutic" session for delving into major cognitive, psychological, or emotional issues. As mentioned earlier in this guidebook, if therapy is truly warranted, both the mentor and mentee should consider referral to a specialized helping professional as the appropriate course of action.

Remember: mutual interest in pursuing complex personal issues within the relationship does not make that pursuit any more acceptable. Both parties must realize that it crosses the proper boundaries of the mentoring model and could result in unanticipated problems rather than desirable solutions. Consequently, no mentor—even the most knowledgeable, conscientious, and skilled—should be viewed as a therapist; and no mentor should be expected to assume, or should mistakenly assume, that he or she has a professional responsibility to enter into the world of therapeutic interaction.

Challenge

For mentor and mentee, the challenge of the confrontative dimension is to examine difficult issues relevant to the purpose of mentoring: to further the mentee's progress toward goal achievement. This examination will move mentees well beyond the information stage, which addresses the issue of *what* they know, to an exchange of viewpoints based on differing perceptions of *how* mentees are putting what they know into practice.

It is the mentor's skill in moving through a serious appraisal of mentee decisions and actions that will determine if they "plateau"—and fixate in the first three stages—or whether they enter the more demanding intellectual, psychological, and emotional territory of the confrontative dimension.

Self-Limiting Mentee Behavior

Mentees need to comprehend the importance of the term *productive* as applied to the mentoring of adult learners. The prefixes *un* and *counter*, when added, respectively, to the word, obviously shift its meaning in significant ways. Less obvious, though, may be what *unproductive* and *counterproductive* mean with regard to self-limiting behavior, and how their definitions illuminate the term *productive* in the context of mentoring.

The Unproductive

An *unproductive* response would be comparable to a mentee action that, although intended to be productive, has no discernible impact or reveals no meaningful increase in positive results. If the mentee's mental outlook is also unaffected by the action, and he or she (like the situation) is not worse off than before, then we can say the action was a *neutral* one. However, we should remember that while it did not cause any noticeable damage, neither did it *advance* the mentee toward goal attainment.

Another scenario is of course possible. Because the mentee anticipated a positive change but none occurred, he or she could develop reservations about, or even experience a loss of confidence in, making further investments of time and energy in the situation. If this development does indeed occur, and the mentee experiences a major backslide of determination, the unproductive action could cross the line into the *counterproductive*.

The Counterproductive

A *counterproductive* action or decision not to act places the mentee squarely in the world of negative consequences because it actually *diminishes* the likelihood of attaining goals. Such consequences can vary from the loss of empirical "things," such as a job promotion, to the loss of inner "reserves," such as self-esteem or professional initiative. The mentee is actually worse off than before because he or she has moved *backward*, away from goal achievement.

To put it in a somewhat dramatic but still relevant way, mentees suffer (at least partially) from "self-inflicted injuries" because they have actually *contributed* to the unfortunate results. In such cases, mentees should expect the issues and problems to be complicated and thus to require serious collaborative attention if workable solutions are to be discovered and applied to the situation.

Timing and Selection

The art of confrontation depends on a combination of mentoring skills, but particularly on the mentor's ability to make constructive decisions about two central, related elements:

1. Timing—*When* to be confrontative

2. Selection—*What* to select as a relevant issue

1. Timing

This involves determining the most likely point during the evolving interpersonal contact when the application of the confrontative dimension might prove beneficial to the mentee. The underlying principle is that mentoring is a dynamic process in which the participants undergo change as a result of successfully moving through various developmental phases within an extended time frame.

Usually the confrontative dimension is introduced into the dialogue *after* the relationship, information, and facilitative phases of mentoring are well underway. The assumption here is that by this time *both* participants will have developed an interpersonal relationship founded on reasonable trust and, as a result, will now be able to handle the difficulties of exploring issues from the confrontative perspective.

Mentees should be aware they can help the mentor by expressing their own willingness to openly examine their past and current effectiveness as problem solvers.

2. Selection

The second element requires astute judgment about whether the specific issue, if raised as a topic of confrontative dialogue, will have a reasonable chance of productive resolution. Selection is based on the following operational assumption: the confrontive dimension will be a valuable collaborative experience if the mentor correctly assesses the *readiness* of the mentee to participate as a constructive individual.

In conclusion, mentees should expect that confrontative interaction will be a respectful attempt to deal with discrepancies revealed by the mentees' avoidance of, or ineffectiveness in dealing with, significant issues related to the attainment of their specific goals. The purpose is to acknowledge there are problems so that workable solutions can be found, *not* to dwell incessantly on past or current errors in judgment. With insight and support, mentees should view their next steps at self-corrective behaviors and initiatives with reasonable confidence.

Dimension 5—Mentor Model

Essential Purpose

The mentor motivates the mentee to take necessary risks (make decisions without certainty of successful results) and to overcome difficulties in his or her own journey toward educational and career goals.

Core Definition

The mentor shares (self-discloses) appropriate life experiences, attitudes, and emotions as a "role model" to the mentee in order to personalize and enrich the relationship.

Mentor Behaviors

- Offer personal thoughts and genuine feelings to emphasize value of work-related learning from unsuccessful or difficult experiences (as trial, error, and self-correction and not as growth-limiting failures).

- Select and relate appropriate examples from own life (and experiences as mentor of other employees) based on probable motivational value.

▪ Provide a direct, positive belief in the mentee through realistic assessment of his or her ability to commit to and achieve attainable goals.

▪ Express a confident view of appropriate "risk-taking" as necessary to pursue opportunities for personal, training, educational, and career development.

▪ Make statements that clearly encourage personal actions toward fulfillment of expressed objectives.

Key Point—MOTIVATION

To understand the interpersonal approach of the mentor model dimension, it is essential to recognize the mentor's central purpose: to motivate and support the mentee's actions. Sometimes this type of motivational effort can even require a necessary "push" in order to move the mentee from a condition of inertia into a position of energized involvement.

Selective Self-Disclosure

One important way mentors attempt to motivate mentees to take current or future risks is by sharing, or self-disclosing, their own comparable life and workplace experiences. Mentors carefully screen these examples beforehand to ensure they are as closely related to the mentee's specific situation as possible; that is, mentors do not randomly select them. If the narratives are to have genuine impact, there must be clear parallels between the mentor and the mentee.

However, mentees also must be aware that sometimes mentors lapse into tales only *they* regard as fascinating and filled with relevant, encouraging messages. In such instances, remember: courteous indulgence has a place. Unless the history becomes an endless monologue, mentees can usually afford to allow mentors to share some fond (albeit unrelated) memories. If the mentor truly believes the story has some direct value for the mentee but the connection is unapparent, then the mentee can politely request a clarification of the point. It is certainly conceivable that with additional explanation the mentor's narrative will reveal a valuable lesson.

Also, mentees should keep in mind that the *details* of the mentor's example do not have to exactly match those of the mentee's situation for the overall point to be relevant. The legitimate value of the comparison may be in how the mentor *thought and felt* about the experience, particularly if this had a positive impact on the mentor's subsequent learning, competence level, and personal and professional confidence. When the mentee is having trouble coping with a very difficult situation, or anticipates having it, such examples can offer precisely the kind of coping strategies and personal encouragement the mentee needs.

References to the Past

Mentees must be prepared for the mentor model dimension because it often involves dealing with a number of sensitive subjects. One in particular is the past—the reservoir of events to which the mentee internally refers for guidance when making decisions in the present. If there is a pronounced history of unsuccessful initiatives, or a record of refusal to pursue uncertain career or academic paths, then it is likely the mentee will have to confront a hard fact: that he or she has drifted into the convenient and comfortable, but unproductive and unfulfilling, terrain of aversion to risk.

Dealing with this aversion is usually not easy for either mentee or mentor, especially if the problem comes as shock to the mentee, is deeply ingrained, or both. For some mentees, the magnetic pull of a "safe" world has become so powerful that minimalizing the chance of "failure" is (by the mentee's conscious choice or not) the dominant agenda. Consequently, mentors often initially face a virtually impenetrable wall of resistance when they suggest a different and more risk-filled course of action.

Mentees must therefore anticipate that in these cases the confrontative aspect of mentoring interaction will be triggered in the mentor model dimension. The need for honest confrontation will be especially acute if mentees are genuinely *unconvinced* that they can trust or rely on their aptitude, stamina, insight, and resources to carry them through demanding or competitive situations. Often, an indicator of this type of mentee problem is an overly vested interest in selecting pursuits that nearly guarantee success.

An individual's rational decision to undertake a career that is consistent with a realistic assessment of his or her strengths and weaknesses is certainly a desirable starting point; from here, though, the individual must be willing to "test" personal abilities. Those mentees who have been reluctant to do so may need to recognize and deal with a disturbing truth: that they may have already denied themselves opportunities for the achievement of attainable objectives because they were more obsessed with the risk of failure than with the probability of success.

Perception of Risk

Whether mentees decide to take risks as necessary to pursue opportunities for career, training, and educational development will depend, to a lesser or greater extent, on their perception of risk, and that in turn will often depend on their past experiences with risk-taking activities.

Mentees who lack an established record of previous accomplishments usually view risk as a major factor in their decision making. They typically are concerned about the cost of failure in terms of rewards (the ends of risk-taking), rather than worried about a loss of time, energy, and finances (the means to those ends). The certainty of task completion, then, is commonly perceived as the major risk factor in mentee decisions of whether or not to move forward and *take the risk*.

However, when mentees have a record of reasonable success, risk may *not* be considered a major factor in the decision-making process. Mentees who have already learned and internalized the value of trial, error, and *self-correction* as an integral component of the learning curve are usually more realistic about accepting risk as a "normal" part of exploring their own talents, and are more resilient when setbacks occur. "Failure" is assumed to be one possible consequence of undertaking new challenges, and the possibility of unsuccessful results is considered an insufficient reason not to pursue meaningful workplace and educational objectives.

Generally, individuals with a healthy perception of risk fully recognize that the path to goal attainment can be strewn with disappointments. Moreover, mentees who have dealt with a failed endeavor usually do not sugarcoat the experience or consider it a trifling event; rather, they tend to acknowledge the sometimes painful but necessary cost of attempting to explore opportunities—with no guarantees of success—in order to discover *what it is realistically possible to achieve in the world*.

Mentees who directly or indirectly communicate that they perceive risk as a central reason to withdraw from situations in which the outcome is uncertain—where success cannot be guaranteed—should therefore anticipate that responsible mentors will raise this perception as a problem in a sensitive and respectful manner.

New Risk versus Old Risk

Mentees with a relatively strong history of demonstrated competency may find that their mentors actively offer encouragement and support not because they believe the mentees are unwilling to take risks, but because the type of risks under review are new and more demanding in practical terms. Usually in such a case, the mentor examines the extent to which the mentee's previous experience can serve as an accurate reference point to guide decisions about current choices.

If the mentor thinks mentees have formed *unrealistic* perceptions about their goals, then mentees may be approached from quite a different direction: the mentor may view risk as an expenditure of important resources that mentees can ill afford to squander.

In these situations, the mentor will attempt to alert the mentee to another extremely important aspect of assessing risk—the probability of *not* attaining the chosen objectives is actually much greater than the mentee understands or recognizes. From the perspective of the mentor, the mentee has minimized, and thus misjudged, the difficulties to be overcome.

Mentees should not be surprised if their reactions to such pointed discussions are sometimes less than enthusiastic; after all, the mentor is raising legitimate issues and posing necessary questions that mentees are expected to address whether they would prefer to do so or not. Although there will probably be some normal tension as a result of such an exchange, mentees should be neither discouraged nor disheartened by the mentor's remarks. Even the most skilled mentoring behavior may not completely smooth the edge of such commentary and feedback.

However, if mentees can accept the mentor's efforts to explore the "risk" of what *may* be an unwise decision, and see it as a chance to participate in a constructive review—and not as an unjustified attempt to challenge their views—then the potential for collaborative, productive dialogue will be greatly increased.

View of the Mentor as Role Model

A role model is someone who is considered worthy of emulation. From the perspective of the mentee, the person "looked up to" is usually one whose behaviors are so special—indicative of personal attributes such as intelligence, psychological stability, and emotional maturity—that they are actually worth copying.

The assumption underlying the selection of mentors is that those who have already distinguished themselves in ways important to the organization are in the best position to serve as guides in the development of less knowledgeable and experienced employees. Often managers are chosen because they have "proven themselves" through professional accomplishments (such as climbing the promotion-advancement ladder), which are regarded as proof that they possess the kind of personal attributes so essential to the mentor as role model.

It is important for mentees to recognize, though, that mentors are not required to be "all things to all people"; mentors do not have to be behavioral paragons in order to exert a positive influence on mentees and illuminate important areas of self-development. Mentees should not hold them to the impossible standard of being perfect role models in all areas of life and work experience. If the mentee benefits reasonably well from participating in a mentoring program, then realistic expectations will have been fulfilled.

Dimension 6—Employee Vision

Essential Purpose

The mentor encourages the mentee to personally initiate constructive change and to productively negotiate through workplace transitions.

Core Definition

The mentor stimulates critical thinking about future careers and reflects on the mentee's plans for developing his or her professional (and personal) potential.

MENTOR BEHAVIORS

- Make statements that require reflection on present and future career, training, and educational attainments.

- Ask questions aimed at clarifying perceptions (positive and negative) about personal ability to manage change.

- Review individual choices based on a reasonable assessment of options and resources.

- Make comments directed at analysis of problem-solving and decision-making strategies.

- Express confidence in carefully thought out decisions.

- Offer remarks that show respect for a mentee's capacity to determine his or her own future.

- Encourage a mentee to develop talents and pursue dreams.

Key Point—INITIATIVE

Mentee vision involves both continuation of self-development and separation from the mentoring program. Ideally, the influence of the mentor as an advocate for mentee development will be "portable" in that the benefits will continue after formal involvement in the mentoring program has concluded.

The mentee, of course, will no longer be in a regular pattern of scheduled meetings with the mentor. While there certainly can be informal interaction (face-to-face or indirect), such contact will tend to be occasional rather than planned. In most instances, the mentee will be like a solo pilot without a mentor copilot sitting nearby as an available resource.

What Mentees Can Expect

Mentees near the point of official separation from the program will usually be fixed on a definite pathway that leads to more imminent as well as later attainments. In anticipating this dimension, mentees can therefore expect the mentor to do the following:

■ Continue to honor the mentees' selected route by actively reviewing their progress, guiding and encouraging them toward the realization of their vision of the future

■ Relate to mentees as serious learners about to "graduate" into a competitive and exciting world of ongoing achievement, disappointment, recovery, assessment, self-correction, and continuing self-initiative

Because the situation of each mentee will differ, mentors will vary in their judgment of what content areas to examine and what types of support to offer in the time remaining. If a number of mentees were to compare the advice given by their respective mentors, most likely they would find that it converges at some points and diverges at others. Such variations underscore the "tailoring" of mentoring to the mentee's needs because mentors will be focusing on the most appropriate of many possible factors, from the degree of mentee commitment given a particular profession to the need for more information before decisions about career and educational pursuits can realistically be determined.

Gaining the Most from This Dimension

If mentees have *any* remaining issues that might be clarified or resolved by the mentoring dialogue, this is the time to raise them. However, it is important that mentees not confuse the official closure of the mentor–mentee relationship with complete resolution of personal or professional concerns and anxieties; as we have seen, the path to self-development (including problem resolution) is ongoing.

In this respect, mentees should regard the mentoring experience as having been a special opportunity for them to travel some of the way—perhaps during an important time of transition—with perceptive guides willing to share their considerable knowledge and experience of the journey, to lend insight into and support for handling the journey's rigors, and even to help the mentee interpret the significance of his or her previous learning.

For some mentees, the most valuable final lesson may simply be in their knowing, and having internalized, that most problems they confront will have workable—if not perfect—solutions as long as they persevere in their efforts to become adept problem solvers.

The experience gained from mentoring can therefore be a vital reference point, because as adult learners, mentees have engaged in two directly related and critical activities:

1. Receiving valuable feedback and guidance focused on their decisions and actions

2. Subsequently demonstrating their individual capability to navigate through change and transition

In essence, mentees will have learned that by successfully dealing with problems, they have earned the right to expect their own individual capacity to pursue learning will continue to be a constructive and reliable compass for future travel.

A Realistic Interpretation of Vision

Although mentoring experiences can vary, one feature usually common to all is the identification, exploration, and implementation of specific learning objectives. As a result of this approach, by the time the employee vision dimension is explored, the mentee's longer-term agenda will have taken on a more definite shape. The vision of the future that the mentee brings to that agenda can be described as:

■ A projected and realistic landscape of fulfilled hopes

■ A "dream" in the meaningful sense of envisioning probable attainments

■ An image of a tangible destination, rather than a vague wish without substantial form and real details

At the beginning of the program, some mentees may quickly show more of an interest in formulating workable strategies to achieve their goals because they have already developed a firm stance regarding their career and academic pursuits; others may be in various stages of certainty about the future, from unsure to almost ready to embark.

Of course, the differences will depend on numerous factors, including the mentee's ability to obtain added information about the details of mandatory job-rotational training (sometimes in other locations), or the need to gather more facts about particular degree-entrance or -completion standards (which may include unanticipated but required courses).

Mentees as Independent Adult Learners

During their evolving relationship, mentor and mentee engage in a serious and often intense collaborative effort to advance the career, training, and educational interests of the mentee, whose own goals are the central focus of mentoring. As the official relationship winds down, both should review and reflect on what the mentee has achieved—and still plans to achieve—as an independent learner.

The mentee will, of course, need to continue making positive initiatives so that longer-term goals will be realized. At this point, a legitimate concern of mentors is the ability of mentees to conduct themselves as adult learners who have benefited from, but not become dependent on, the mentoring relationship as a primary source of counsel and support.

Relevance of a Network

Considering the above, mentees should not be surprised by questions regarding their implementation and maintenance of a current network of resources that can provide reasonable assistance if needed. In some cases, such a reliable framework of assistance may already be in place.

As separation gradually occurs, mentees will increasingly need to shift away from reliance on a collaborative model to a view of themselves as the primary source of cognitive decision-making and problem-solving strategies. Moreover, mentees will need to accept the sometimes uncomfortable reality that there will be limited or indirect psychological and emotional support from others, and that they will not be able to count on the positive reinforcement of mentor-mentee dialogue. Having an intact network of resources can bolster a mentee's confidence in this respect.

Such a network is clearly a valuable asset, then, especially for mentees who are appropriately reliant on others for various forms of assistance.

Change and Transition

The mentee vision dimension is the final element of mentor concern. Mentees should consider the changes that occurred through the experience of personal growth as encouraging signs for the future and their successful transition to more independent learning.

- Mentees entered the mentoring model of learning as unique individuals with varying perceptions, aptitudes, needs, experiences, and objectives. Ideally, they found mentors who adjusted the individual practice of the model to their mentees' unique needs and personalities in order to best serve their specific interests as adults committed to professional development and achievement.

- The one-to-one relationship probably involved specific orientations, seminars, and training workshops, including recommended publications for both mentor and mentee to use as constructive guides to promote their involvement as knowledgeable participants. These forms of information likely enriched the mentoring relationship.

- Mentees who began in an optimum position—who were secure about their choices, had resolved the important issues requiring hard facts, and were well underway to attaining their goals—may have needed less attention devoted to their knowledge-base and been more focused on the support component of mentoring—the mentor as resource and guide regarding psychological and emotional concerns. Mentees who needed such "tailoring" most likely increased their confidence and now are ready to actually reach those goals.

- Mentees who entered the program with uncertainties about their goals or with vague goals are probably on firmer ground now, with a changed perspective of goals and a fuller understanding of the need for clear and realistic goal definition. They should not be surprised to discover that they also benefited from the "support" component, especially as the expected but still difficult stress and strain of the journey gathered cumulative weight.

The employee vision dimension can be viewed as a trip with a future destination that depends to a significant degree on the *initial vision* and often *changed perspective* of the adult learner who is the primary traveler.

CONCLUSION

Mentor and Mentee Preparation

Professionals who have made the commitment to serve as mentors can refer to published materials that will aid them in translating their good intentions into competent mentoring behaviors. Self-assessment inventories and books devoted to the subject of mentoring adult learners have increasingly been used by sponsors of organized programs as an integral component of orientations, seminars, and workshop training sessions.

Mentees as well can prepare themselves, so they can take maximum advantage of the opportunities offered by mentoring programs. By engaging in preliminary and ongoing self-directed education relevant to the one-to-one model of learning, they can increase their capacity to respond as constructive participants (1) upon entering into the initial phase of mentoring relationships, and (2) during their full involvement as adult learners with their mentors.

With both the mentee and the mentor assuming collaborative responsibility from the very start of their contact, the mentee will be in an even more favorable position to benefit from face-to-face learning in the workplace.

Remembering the Mentee's Responsibilities

Although mentors are considered to be primary influences on the success of the mentoring program, mentees should remember they are major contributors to the quality and value of the mentoring experience as well. The final results of the program—mentee career and academic progress—will ultimately depend on the mentor's behavioral skills and the mentee's ability to share as an enlightened and active partner in the complex process of evolving mentor–mentee dialogue and activity.

It is in this cooperative spirit that mentees correctly make the decision to undertake the journey with a mentor. Fortunately, the great majority of mentees approach their mentors as highly important sources of guidance and support, not as miracle workers who are somehow expected to transform unwilling or resistant individuals into career or academic successes within a limited span of time.

Mentees must be prepared to function as fully engaged adult learners, given (1) the realistic limits in resources and personnel available, even in mentoring programs with ambitious agendas and conscientious staff, and (2) the appropriate expectation by mentors of sincere and noteworthy reciprocity from those selected as mentees.

The extent of the mentees' preparation, level of active involvement, and continuing efforts to improve their proficiencies as collaborative participants will all be critical factors in the specific relevance for them of the mentoring opportunity as a benchmark experience. Certainly, mentees have a legitimate personal and professional interest in the outcome.

As mentees who have been successfully mentored increasingly assume their own role as mentors, the mentoring model can truly become a viable option for adults in our society who want to experience the rich potential of one-to-one learning.

APPENDICES

Contents

APPENDIX A. *Summary of the Complete Mentor Role*

APPENDIX B. *Behavioral Profile of an Effective Mentee*

Use of the Appendices

Mentees can use Appendix A and B in two ways:

1. *To prepare for the mentoring session.* Before each session, mentees can easily review the mentor's complete role by referring to Appendix A. They also can increase their readiness to respond as productive participants by referring to the behavioral profile in Appendix B (also presented as Figure 1 in Chapter 5).

2. *To reflect on the mentoring session.* After each session, mentees can use the appendices as joint guides for reflecting on the evolving mentoring relationship's personal and professional significance for them.

Mentees should accompany the post-session use of the appendices with an effort to maintain their mentee journal (see Chapter 3). By also having a written record of each session, mentees can more accurately monitor the significance of the ongoing interpersonal interaction and activities as factors in genuine contributions to their career, training, and educational development.

Appendix A   Summary of the Complete Mentor Role

Dimension 1. RELATIONSHIP

- KEY POINT—*Trust*
- Responsive Listening
- Open-Ended Questions
- Descriptive Feedback
- Perception Checks
- Nonjudgmental Responses

Dimension 2. INFORMATION

- KEY POINT—*Advice*
- Questions about Present
- Review of Background
- Probing Questions
- Directive Comments
- Restatements
- Reliance on Facts

Dimension 3. FACILITATIVE

- KEY POINT—*Alternatives*
- Hypothetical Questions
- Uncovering Assumptions
- Multiple Viewpoints
- Examining Commitment
- Analysis of Reasons
- Review of Preferences

Dimension 4. CONFRONTATIVE

- KEY POINT—*Challenge*
- Careful Probing
- Open Acknowledgment
- Assessment of Discrepancies
- Selective Behaviors
- Attention to Feedback
- Comments about Potential

Dimension 5. MENTOR MODEL

- KEY POINT—*Motivation*
- Offering Thoughts and Feelings
- Selecting Related Examples
- Realistic Belief in Ability
- Confident View of Risk
- Statements about Action

Dimension 6. EMPLOYEE VISION

- KEY POINT—*Initiative*
- Reflection on Present/Future
- Questions about Change
- Review of Choices
- Comments about Strategies
- Expressions of Confidence
- Respect for Abilities
- Encouragement for Dreams

MENTOR BEHAVIORS

MENTEE BEHAVIORS

1. RELATIONSHIP: Key Point—Trust

- Shares and reflects on experiences
- Listens empathetically
- Understands and accepts

- Offers Detailed Explanations
- Expects Mentor to Listen and to Ask Questions

2. INFORMATION Key Point—Advice

- Offers facts about career, education, plans, progress
- Comments about use of information
- Exhibits tailored, accurate, and sufficient knowledge

- Provides Facts and Records
- Expects Mentor to Review Use and Depth of Sources

3. FACILITATIVE Key Point—Alternatives

- Explores interests, abilities, ideas, beliefs
- Provides other views/attainable goals
- Shares personal decisions about career, training, education

- Explains Choices and Decisions
- Expects Mentor to Pose Options and Other Views

4. CONFRONTATIVE Key Point—Challenge

- Shows respect for decisions, actions, career
- Shares insight into counterproductive strategies and behaviors
- Evaluates need and capacity to change

- Reflects on Initiatives
- Expects Mentor to Examine Goals and Approach

5. MENTOR MODEL: Key Point—Motivation

- Discloses life experience as role model
- Personalizes and enriches relationship
- Takes risks; Overcomes difficulties in education and career

- Expresses Main Concerns
- Expects Mentor to Share Ideas and Feelings

6. EMPLOYEE VISION: Key Point—Initiative

- Thinks critically about career future
- Considers personal/professional potential
- Initiates change; Negotiates transitions

- Visualizes Own Future
- Expects Mentor to Examine Plans and Encourage Progress